A Denouement

Jennifer Murray

BookLeaf Publishing

India | USA | UK

Presentation by *BookLeaf Publishing*

Web: www.bookleafpub.com

E-mail: info@bookleafpub.com

ISBN: 9789357215701

First edition 2022

*To my wonderful husband for never hesitating
to encourage me to follow my wildest dreams
and deepest desires, and for loving me the way
you do. ttbt*

*For my delightful two daughters who bring so
much joy to my life. Mom loves you both so
much, and I am blessed to be your mother.
Since I knew of your existence, my heart and
life has been yours.*

*To my parents for their unwavering belief in me,
my intelligence and my talent. But most of all,
for their love. If I am half the parent the two of
you were, I will consider myself a success.*

*To my personal hero, my big sister. I have
looked up to you for three and a half decades,
there is little point in stopping now.*

*To my fantastic nephews: you were the first
babies I ever helped care for, and you are
growing to be incredible human beings.*

*To my in-laws for welcoming me into the family
with open on and becoming a second set of*

parents to me. I cannot overstate how much your support and love has meant and will always mean to me.

To all of my friends who are like family.

I love you all.

PREFACE

My life, like most others, has not been one free from loss.

I think over the course of time I grew terrified of forging connections just for a tragic ending to come along. From death, to betrayal, to unbridled joy, it is all here.

My hope is that my work helps someone else realize there are plenty of quirky people like themselves a lot sooner than I did.

Triumph Through Connection

Beyond the hopelessness
and devastation
lies a brighter future.
Where we all join hands,
conquering injustices
after realizing
we became so connected
it caused disconnect.
But now we can forge
stronger bonds than before
then give thanks
when we emerge
VICTORIOUS.

LEH

2

It started with
Burnt cds
And blew up from there
Now you're the person I talk about least
But you haven't gone anywhere

Thank the Gods we made it out alive
Scenes from an Italian restaurant
Replay all the time
When you had all of me
And you were mine

Whips and knives
Whispers and promises
They still eat me alive
Flashbacks to a wooden playground
And simpler times

Songbird

For a moment,
She felt like she dodged a bullet.
Not a single song on her list was selected.
Then at the last minute,
The room shifted and the floor gave out.
Of course, of all the songs available,
What was chosen was the one being done as a
favor.

Songs can be funny like that,
Sometimes what or whom they are associated
with
Dictates if you love it or if you despise it.

This song once brought joy to her,
Because she believed what she was singing.
Now she avoids it the same way she avoids all
the places that haunt her.

She says nothing, long ago resigning herself to
her fate, but her mind screams in protest.
"I said I was a singer, not an actress!"
The words echo in her head unspoken
While she sits with a smile plastered on.

Letting artificial warmth thaw the ice now
resting in her chest.
"It's going to be so much fun!" is what she
settles on.

A half truth, really.
Her father would say she was lying by omission,
But this is what she does:
Puts herself in situations that make her deeply
uncomfortable out of love...
Or out of complete lack of self-respect.

Because she is excited about the music,
Even excited to sing...
But she's a bird who loathes enclosures,
And can't sing while confined to a cage.

She needs space
Enough to hold all the emotion that is released

She assumes she can overcome it,
A song is just a song, after all.
Unless it isn't.

The four weeks following are a haze
Of pressing play to practice
And not even making it through the first chorus.
Frozen in shock, her daily attempts are useless.

Out of desperation,
She kneels at her altar,
Making offering after offering,
Praying for strength.
Praying for the emotional bleeding to be
cauterized.

She crawls into bed and awaits an answer.
She wakes, mind split open because she now
understood
The cage was in her mind.

The day arrives and she is filled with tranquility
She had never known before.
She opens her mouth and does what her father
abhors:
Lies by omission.
Because she still does not believe a word she is
singing.

Love

Love is here
Love lights the world
Love sings
Love is who you know
Love is weird
Love hurts
Love is suicide
Love is like a role that we play
Love is all you need
Loving you is loving me

Labyrinths

Spiral out
to
Spiral back
to center

to home
to truth
to stripped-down self

trip one
in a church
whilst vacationing

I took those
who matter most
to walk at LEAF

While I was
Spiraling out
Not quite ready to
Spiral back to center

Instead allowing
Labyrinths and good people
To anchor me

to home
to truth
to love
to self

Smells Like Home

the quiet stomping
of hooves.
the smell of hay,
cut apples and carrots.

gentle whinnies
to loud neighs
long-lashed eyes
whiskered chins

leather saddles
thick blankets
the scent of fly spray
wafting through
the tacking area.

the unmistakable
smell of the arena,
fresh sawdust strewn around.
the feel of it
through your boots
on the ground.

for horse lovers,
the barn smells...

like home.

The Call

A corner shop
with a rack of crystals.
A young version of myself
marveling over them all,
Convincing my mother
I needed an Amethyst pocket rock.
Carefully giving it
a nail-polish smile
once safely home.

Playing with a
neighbor girl
sitting beneath
my families dining room window.
Grounded in dirt
attempting to
cast spells,
contact Spirits.

A corner shop
with glass display cases.
Overflowing with crystal jewelry
organized by astrological sign.
Purchases still beloved
over a decade later:

Trusty rutilated quartz ring
Fairy tie-dye dress
and
A blue kyanite pendant,
which now adorns our wedding besom.

Sitting in a dive bar
having my cards read
for the very first time.
For one reason or another,
it feels less intimidating
than a traditional reading.
I quietly promise myself
I will one day learn
to read my own.

Dragging both
friends and lovers
to my favorite museum,
for purely selfish reasons.
Getting lost
in the gem room,
stunned by the entire display.
Artful lighting.
Floating glass shelves.
The specimens' sheer beauty
commanding my attention.
Swearing
I would have a private collection

someday.
Still not understanding
WHY they had such
a magnetic pull,

which is why
my friend's video shoot there
felt obscene.

Standing on
the deck of a bar,
staring out
into the woods ahead.
Being instructed
about shadow people,
learning to charge crystals,
discovering I held
POWER.
A mentor
that vanished completely.
Untraceable.
No more.

My first crystal wand,
shipped long distance.
A labradorite dream,
with flash that left me
completely mesmerized.
A purchase made in secrecy,

the transaction itself
a quiet rebellion.
During a time
I was finally breaking free
from the chains
I had wrapped around myself.
A sadistic security blanket of sorts.

A first date
that altered reality.
Falling to my knees
in front of a shelf
lined with crystals
instead of DVDs.
I had previously marveled
at men with actual bookshelves,
but never crystals.
This particular display
had me staring at him
mouth agape
thoroughly dumbfounded,
more than intrigued,
suddenly mildly aroused.

First trip
to a metaphysical shop
in the place
I now call home.
The place

I would purchase
my first deck from -
the second stage
in the rebellion.

Date night
with my future husband
to his favorite shop,
the place we now select
anniversary gifts from.

A wedding
on the Winter Solstice,
to my divine masculine.
Waltzing into that
treasured storefront
still dressed in wedding attire.
Being told
I looked like Cinderella
in the first dress
I've ever loved.

A grandmother
who became the first person
to directly ask
if I was a witch.
The gift of a cauldron
that now sits
beside the altar

I share with her grandson.

Picture of ancestors
that adorn our space.
Talking to ghosts.
Praying for guidance,
from those we've lost.

Remaining grounded.
Remaining true.

Denied Desire

Stolen glances
Unrequited love
Denied desire
due to insecurity
self-loathing
fear

At a time
I was primarily
attracted to females
I ran
I buried
I hid

Higher standards
for women versus men.
A lifetime of rejection
leaving me paralyzed.

Hotels

Clandestine meeting
to retrieve a shirt
transforms into
an illicit rendezvous
shrouded in betrayal.
Blinded by naivete,
my transgressions
the lesser between us.
Myself
an unknowing accomplice.

Intoxicated.
Bored.
Self-destructive.
The only excuses.

But even they cannot
explain away my shame.

Prior to that
a first kiss
that was forced upon me,
pinned beneath
an overeager teenager.

Blindsided
he became my first boyfriend.
The first time
I embraced a toxic partner.
The one who set the tone.

Affirmation

Rolling over
to spy a nefarious text.
The sender
feeling the fact
they had dreamt of me
appropriate to share.

Confusion
Then shock
Utter disbelief
of the audacity
the sheer hubris at hand

Sympathy for him
Clearly cracking
Under the strain of fatherhood
Haunted by the shadows
remaining from the work
he's so long avoided.

Anger at his hypocrisy,
the knowledge
that he remains him
regardless of his
carefully constructed image.

Each contact
bringing the opportunity
To show gratitude to myself
For walking away from that man
all those years ago.

Campfire Tears

former partner
ugly crying
mid-coitus
over his own sins
his own questionable choices

half-heartedly comforting him
staring into the flames
watching my resolve grow

him unaware
he had never lost me

I was never his
in the first place.

Cabin Living

gathering water from a well
boiling it to wash dishes
a woodstove the only heat source
a winter spent reflecting
still refusing to simply go home
to warmth
to fire
to love

I struggled
solely because of pride.

shivering in a cold cabin
with no mailing address
calling it a dwelling
when it was quicksand.

Grounding

24

almost from birth
wild and untamed
picking berries
pretending back yard hedges
concealed a
secret garden sanctuary

an old well in the woods
so long forgotten
marveling at discarded
household treasures

running over trails
breathing in the smells
enjoying nature's symphony

a ritual by a tree
dear friend by my side
us removing our shackles together

a witchling daughter
who keeps an altar in her room
following her mother's footsteps
unafraid to embrace herself

what I could not give to myself
I have given to her

25

Moments

copper coin
omni
Cleveland
and a swanky bar

Valentine's
Indian buffet
double date
absinthe
billiards

A little person
descending a pole
pouring shots
into open mouths

Deception
Disconnect
Distrust

Modern romance
at its finest

Skywatcher

27

strewn across a hill
tall blades of grass
tickling my back

counting clouds
naming shapes
setting intentions
for a life still to come

charging crystals
conducting rituals
to unlock
secret knowledge
held in the heaven's above.

Letting Go

over the course of time
my resolve
gradually weakened

life chipped away
enough of my armor
to leave me
weak
defenseless
uncaring
numb

I was all too relieved
to slip beneath the waves

Avoidance

a desire to be liked
coupled with social anxiety
filling perceived silence
with senseless chatter
annoying even myself

either caring too much
or not at all
no gray area to be seen

cancelling plans
burrowing beneath blankets
unanswered attempts at contact
avoidance by design

PAHC

standing on a balcony
friend beside me
watching the floor
erupt into chaos and violence

loyalty and love at its core
misfits
the misunderstood
creating their own
safe haven
escape

past the mule kicks
and flying fists
beneath the screams

love
serenity
a place I always felt
safe

Too Much

too intelligent
too talkative
too much in general

too weird
too outspoken
too energetic
too much as a whole

statements
used to describe me
in the end,
words that shattered me

I retreated within
cocooning myself
in a cacophony of criticism
I transformed
a hull of who I had been

dumbed down speech
frivolous talking points
quiet and reserved
slowing down
editing my very essence

for approval

but one can only
suppress themselves
for so long
before true self
breaks free

unabashedly myself
but now mindful
of the company I keep

Home sick

seven years out
still missing home
the winters
the museums
the lack of seasonal allergies

unable
to fully let go
and embrace my new life
forget all I left behind

A Life Saved

ill-equipped
to express myself
audibly

I resorted to
letting the emotion out
when it became
overwhelming

the sight of
my own blood
the only thing
to calm me

every failure
every rejection
every misstep
an excuse

to enter the bathtub
listen to music
begin my abuse

a New Year's Promise
to a suicidal best friend

to stop
to never pick up a blade again
a promise I kept
regardless of what life threw my way
a promise I have managed
to keep to this day